GET THE ANSWERS! HISTORY

Q&A ABOUT SLAVERY IN AMERICA

By Benjamin Proudfit

INVESTIGATE!

Enslow PUBLISHING

Please visit our website, www.enslow.com. For a free color catalog of all our high-quality books, call toll free 1-800-398-2504 or fax 1-877-980-4454.

Library of Congress Cataloging-in-Publication Data

Names: Proudfit, Benjamin author
Title: Q & A about slavery in America / Benjamin Proudfit.
Other titles: Questions and answers about slavery in America
Description: Buffalo, New York : Enslow Publishing, [2026] | Series: Get the answers!: history | Includes index. | Audience term: juvenile | Audience: Grades 2-3 Enslow Publishing
Identifiers: LCCN 2024050793 (print) | LCCN 2024050794 (ebook) | ISBN 9781978544314 (library binding) | ISBN 9781978544307 (paperback) | ISBN 9781978544321 (ebook)
Subjects: LCSH: Slavery–United States–Miscellanea–Juvenile literature
Classification: LCC E441 .P97 2026 (print) | LCC E441 (ebook) | DDC 306.3/620973–dc23/eng/20241114
LC record available at https://lccn.loc.gov/2024050793
LC ebook record available at https://lccn.loc.gov/2024050794

Published in 2026 by
Enslow Publishing
2544 Clinton Street
Buffalo, NY 14224

Copyright © 2026 Enslow Publishing

Designer: Andrea Davison-Bartolotta
Editor: Kristen Nelson

Photo credits: Cover, pp. 1, 6, 7, 8, 10, 12, 13, 15, 16, 27 Everett Collection/Shutterstock.com; series art (question mark backgrounds) Darcraft/Shutterstock.com; pp. 4, 5, 9, 11 (Jefferson), 14, 17 courtesy of Library of Congress; pp. 11 (Franklin, Madison, Jay), 18, 23 National Portrait Gallery, Smithsonian Institution; p. 20 Gift of Erving and Joyce Wolf, in memory of Diane R. Wolf, 1982/The Metropolitan Museum of Art; p. 21 U.S. National Park Service; p. 22 File:Chickamauga.jpg/Wiimedia Commons; p. 24 U.S. Army; p. 25 National Archives; p. 26 Biden White House Archived/Flickr; p. 28 Wirestock Creators/Shutterstock.com; p. 29 (bottom) ryanbphotography/Shutterstock.com; p. 29 (top) Monkey Business Images/Shutterstock.com.

All rights reserved. No part of this book may be reproduced in any form without permission in writing from the publisher, except by a reviewer.

Printed in the United States of America

Some of the images in this book illustrate individuals who are models. The depictions do not imply actual situations or events.

CPSIA compliance information: Batch #CS26ENS: For further information contact Enslow Publishing, at 1-800-398-2504.

Find us on

CONTENTS

A Matter of Race 4

From Native Americans to Africans. 6

Slavery in Early America 9

An Enslaved Life................................. 12

The Growing Divide.............................. 16

The Civil War 22

Abolishing Slavery...............................25

Racism Today...................................28

Glossary 30

For More Information 31

Index 32

Words in the glossary appear in **bold** type the first time they are used in the text.

A MATTER OF RACE

When Americans talk about slavery in our country, they mean the buying, selling, and forced work of Africans and their **descendants**. However, people have been enslaving others for hundreds of years, including in Africa and Europe.

Slavery in North America was based on white people believing they were better than Black people. Many thought they had the right to own the Black people they enslaved. The practice led to **racism** that Black Americans still fight against today.

"Slave" is a word that was used for a long time. Today, "enslaved person" is a better way to talk about those who were forced into work without pay. It reminds us that they were people.

FROM NATIVE AMERICANS TO AFRICANS

QUESTION 1

Who were the first enslaved people?

ANSWER

The first people enslaved by Europeans in the Western **Hemisphere** were Native peoples. **Explorer** Christopher Columbus enslaved Native Americans in the 1490s. The Queen of Spain later said to stop. The Spanish enslaved Native people in Puerto Rico too.

This image from 1595 shows the Spanish enslaving Native people they met.

QUESTION 2

When did enslaved people from Africa come to North America?

••••• ANSWER •••••

A group of Africans who reached North America in 1619 are often said to be the first enslaved people. They were on a Portuguese ship headed for Mexico. Pirates stopped the ship and took the enslaved people to a port near Jamestown.

Jamestown (present-day Virginia) was the first lasting British settlement. The enslaved people brought there were from Angola, a country in Africa.

QUESTION 3

What was the slave trade?

ANSWER

It was the buying and selling of people who had been enslaved. Ships brought enslaved people from Africa to North America, South America, and the Caribbean. Conditions on these ships were bad. Many Africans died before they reached where they were going.

ship carrying enslaved people

SLAVERY IN EARLY AMERICA

QUESTION 4

Did enslaved people take part in the American Revolution?

ANSWER

Yes. In 1775, there were more than 500,000 enslaved people living in the 13 British colonies. Many fought as part of the colonial army, hoping to win their freedom just as the white colonists did.

In general, enslavers in the Southern colonies did not let their enslaved people fight in the American Revolution, which took place from 1775 to 1781.

QUESTION 5

Did the Founding Fathers own enslaved people?

ANSWER

Yes. These men worked hard to gain the colonies' independence from Great Britain. But, at the time, the famous words of the Declaration of Independence—that "all men are created equal"—didn't include enslaved people. In fact, four of the first five U.S. presidents were enslavers.

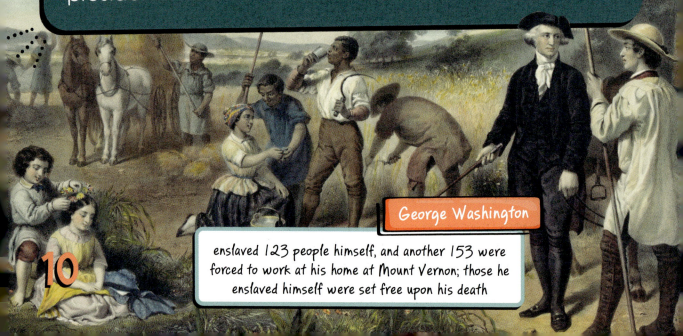

George Washington enslaved 123 people himself, and another 153 were forced to work at his home at Mount Vernon; those he enslaved himself were set free upon his death

Founding Enslavers

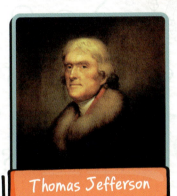
Thomas Jefferson

enslaved more than 600 people at his home, Monticello, and other properties over the course of his life; tried to **condemn** the trade of enslaved people in the Declaration of Independence but it was cut out

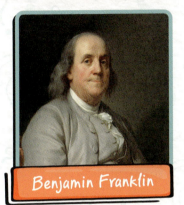
Benjamin Franklin

enslaved at least seven people over many years; late in life spoke out against slavery; did not own any enslaved people when he died

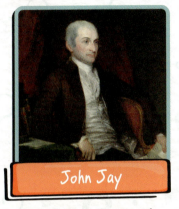
John Jay

enslaved about 17 people; came from a family of enslavers; founded an antislavery group in New York in 1785

Many Founding Fathers were enslavers. Some, like Benjamin Franklin and John Jay, started to speak out against slavery later in their lives.

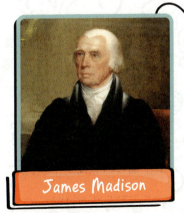
James Madison

enslaved more than 100 people; **criticized** slavery and the trade of enslaved people many times; brought enslaved people to work at the White House when he was president

11

AN ENSLAVED LIFE

QUESTION 6

What kinds of work were enslaved people forced to do?

ANSWER

As most enslaved people lived in the American South, many worked on large farms called plantations. They planted and harvested crops such as tobacco and rice. They also worked in homes cooking, cleaning, and caring for their enslavers' children.

In 1808, a law ended any trade in enslaved people between the United States and other countries. However, trade of enslaved people still happened within the United States for many years.

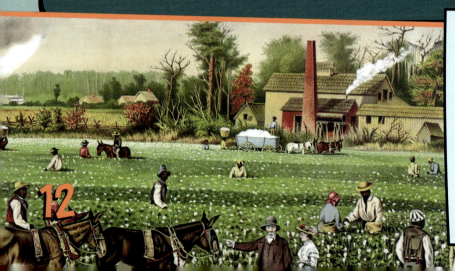

QUESTION 7

How were enslaved people treated?

••••• **ANSWER** •••••

Enslaved people had awful living conditions and food. They were beaten. They were forced to work long hours doing back-breaking labor. Most slaves were kept from learning to read or write. This made them **dependent** on their enslavers.

Families of enslaved people were separated when members were sold. They may have been sold in **auctions** like the one shown here.

QUESTION 8

Did enslaved people ever rebel against their enslavers?

ANSWER

Yes, many times. An enslaved man named Nat Turner led a rebellion in Virginia in 1831. He killed the family that enslaved him, gathered a group of other enslaved people, and killed many more white people.

Nat Turner's Rebellion made enslavers even more fearful of what would happen if enslaved people came together to fight against their enslavement.

QUESTION 9

How many enslaved people lived in the United States?

ANSWER

By 1810, more than 1.1 million people were enslaved in the United States. About 4 million enslaved people lived in the United States by 1860! At that point, more than 55 percent of the population of the state of Mississippi was enslaved people.

THE GROWING DIVIDE

QUESTION 10

What part did slavery play in the Southern economy?

ANSWER

By 1860, the United States produced two-thirds of the world's cotton. This was possible because of the millions of enslaved people working in cotton fields and production. The South made a lot of money because of their enslaved workers.

QUESTION 11

Was there slavery in the North?

••••• **ANSWER** •••••

Yes, though the number of enslaved people in the North was never as high as in the South. Northern businessmen put their money into the trade of enslaved people and the plantations they worked on. In that way, many people in the North kept slavery going too.

Though there were fewer enslaved people in the North, there was still racism against African Americans. Even if they weren't enslaved, they were treated poorly.

QUESTION 12

Who were the abolitionists?

ANSWER

Abolitionists were people who wanted to abolish, or get rid of, slavery altogether. Frederick Douglass was an abolitionist who had once been enslaved and escaped. He traveled around the country speaking about abolishing slavery.

Frederick Douglass

Abolition in the United States Before the Civil War

1777: Vermont ends enslavement for men over age 21 and women over age 18.

1780: A Pennsylvania law sets up a **gradual** abolition of slavery.

1783: Slavery is abolished in Massachusetts through the courts.

1802: Ohio becomes a state. The state **constitution** outlaws slavery.

1804: All states north of Maryland have passed laws abolishing or gradually abolishing slavery.

1816: Indiana becomes a state. The state constitution outlaws slavery.

1846: Iowa becomes a state. Slavery is not allowed.

1848: Illinois rewrites its constitution to abolish slavery.

1850: California becomes a state. The state constitution outlaws slavery.

1861: Kansas becomes a state. Slavery is not allowed.

Before the Civil War, many northern states and new states had begun abolishing slavery. However, most places didn't do away with slavery all at once.

QUESTION 13

Did enslaved people try to escape?

····· ANSWER ·····

Some enslaved people tried, though it was dangerous. They had to leave their family behind. They didn't know what awaited them as they fled. They might not have food, face bad weather, or worst of all, be caught.

In the mid-1800s, there were laws allowing people to catch an enslaved person who ran away and return them to their enslaver.

QUESTION 14

What was the Underground Railroad?

••••• **ANSWER** •••••

It was a network of people, **routes**, and places that helped enslaved people find freedom. People of all kinds helped freedom seekers on the Underground Railroad, including former enslaved people and other free Black Americans.

Freedom seekers didn't just head North. They journeyed to Canada, Mexico, West, and beyond to Europe! The red arrows show the many routes of the Underground Railroad.

THE CIVIL WAR

QUESTION 15

Did slavery cause the Civil War?

ANSWER

Most historians agree the divide between the North and South on the subject of slavery was a main cause of the Civil War. States' rights and westward growth also played a part, but these were also tied to slavery.

The Civil War was a war between the United States (North) and 11 states that left the union to become the Confederate States of America (South). It took place from 1861 to 1865.

QUESTION 16

What was the Emancipation Proclamation?

ANSWER

President Abraham Lincoln put out this proclamation, or announcement, on January 1, 1863. It said that all enslaved people in the Confederacy were free. However, in most cases, in order for these people to get their freedom, United States troops had to win battles in their area!

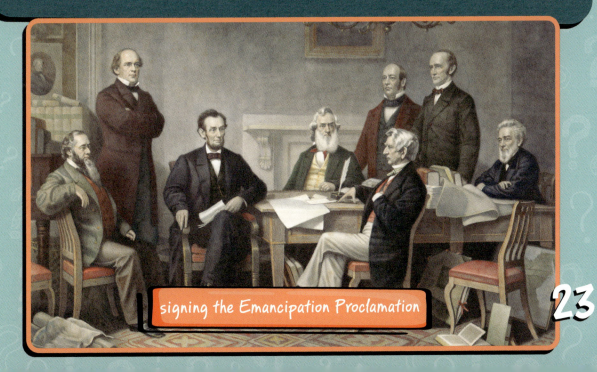

signing the Emancipation Proclamation

QUESTION 17

Did enslaved people fight in the Civil War?

ANSWER

Formerly enslaved people living in the North were allowed to join U.S. troops shortly before 1863. Then, the Emancipation Proclamation said the freed enslaved people in Confederate states could join U.S. troops. Many did.

About 180,000 Black men joined the United States troops in the Civil War. Many were formerly enslaved.

24

ABOLISHING SLAVERY

QUESTION 18

How did slavery end in the United States?

ANSWER

The 13th Amendment to the U.S. Constitution abolished slavery in the United States. It was ratified, or officially agreed to, on December 6, 1865. It was the first of three amendments that gave civil rights to all Americans, including people who were formerly enslaved.

An amendment is a change or addition to a constitution.

QUESTION 19

What does Juneteenth have to do with slavery?

ANSWER

Juneteenth celebrates June 19, 1865. This is the day the enslaved people in Galveston, Texas, found out they were free. News moved slower in those days. Confederate states like Texas hadn't made the Emancipation Proclamation known to the enslaved people in their states.

President Joe Biden made Juneteenth a national holiday in 2021.

QUESTION 20

What happened to enslaved people after they were freed?

ANSWER

In the South, many formerly enslaved people became sharecroppers. Sharecropping is when someone rents land, gear, and other needed items from a landlord. However, some enslaved people were able to go to school. Others got jobs with the U.S. government.

Sharecropping wasn't much better for Black Americans than slavery.

RACISM TODAY

Even though slavery was abolished, racism continued. Black Americans faced unequal treatment and unfair laws for another 100 years. The civil rights movement, which happened in the 1950s and 1960s, helped Black Americans gain many of the rights they had been promised.

However, Black Americans are still met with racism and unfair treatment today. Movements like Black Lives Matter work to call attention to this treatment. They try to get better laws passed and set up programs to help the United States have true equality for all.

In many places in the United States, Black Americans are still fighting for the rights they gained as U.S. citizens in the 13th Amendment.

29

GLOSSARY

auction: A sale of goods or property at which buyers bid against one another for items.

condemn: To say strongly that something is wrong.

constitution: The basic laws by which a country or state is governed.

criticize: To express disapproval of someone or something.

dependent: Needing someone else for help or support.

descendant: A person who is related to someone who lived in the past.

economy: The money made in an area and how it is made.

explorer: One who comes to a place to find new things.

gradual: Happening in a slow way over a period of time.

hemisphere: One half of Earth.

racism: The belief that people of different races have different qualities and abilities that are superior or inferior.

rebel: To fight to overthrow a government.

route: A path to follow.

For More Information

Books

Alexander, Kwame. *Unspoken: Talking About Slavery*. London, UK: Andersen Press, 2023.

Dockery, Patricia Williams. *Slavery and the African American Story*. New York, NY: Crown Books for Young Readers, 2023.

Wesgate, Kathryn. *Uncovering the History of Slavery at Mount Vernon*. New York, NY: Enslow Publishing, 2023.

Websites

Colonial America: Slavery
https://www.ducksters.com/history/colonial_america/slavery.php
Find out more about slavery in early America here.

Slavery
https://kids.britannica.com/kids/article/slavery/353782
Learn more about the history of slavery here.

Publisher's note to educators and parents: Our editors have carefully reviewed these websites to ensure that they are suitable for students. Many websites change frequently, however, and we cannot guarantee that a site's future contents will continue to meet our high standards of quality and educational value. Be advised that students should be closely supervised whenever they access the internet.

INDEX

abolition, 18, 19, 25, 28

Africans, 4, 7, 8

Black Lives Matter, 28

civil rights movement, 28

Civil War, 19, 22, 24

Columbus, Christopher, 6

Confederate States of America, 22, 23, 24, 26

Declaration of Independence, 10, 11

Douglass, Frederick, 18

Emancipation Proclamation, 23, 24, 26

Founding Fathers, 10, 11

Juneteenth, 26

Lincoln, Abraham, 23

Native people, 6

Nat Turner's Rebellion, 14

plantation, 12, 17

population of enslaved people, 15

racism, 4, 17, 28

slave trade, 8, 11, 12, 17

13th Amendment, 25, 29

Underground Railroad, 21